27 C0-AHH 725

EIGHT CRITICAL LEADERSHIP SKILLS
CREATED THROUGH EFFECTIVE DIVERSITY PARTNERSHIPS:
A SKILLS-BUILDING FIELD GUIDE

By: Michael Welp, Jo Ann Morris and Bill Proudman

WMFDP, LLC

Copyright © 2005 by WMFDP, LLC
First Edition
All rights reserved. No part of this book may be reproduced or transmitted in any form by any means, electronic or mechanical, including photocopying, recording or by any information storage and retrieval system, without written permission from the publisher, except for the inclusion of brief quotations in reviews and certain other non-commercial uses permitted by copyright law. For permission requests, write to the publisher, addressed "Attention: Permission Coordinator," at the address below.

WMFDP, LLC
PO Box 12436
Portland, OR 97212
(503) 281-5585

Order books at www.wmfdp.com

ISBN 0-9754192-0-X
Library of Congress Control Number: 2004107088

TESTIMONIALS

"Proudman, Welp and Morris have very effectively translated into print their profound work in diversity partnerships. They've described the complex humanity involved in leadership in crisp phrases with great clarity. The reflective questions will surely enable the reader to connect head with heart to truly achieve personal growth in partnering for diversity."

Lars Houmann
Executive Vice President and Chief Operating Officer
Florida Hospital

"This excellent series, on fostering skill-building in partnership surrounding diversity issues, is practical and relevant for both genders and for interfacing with all races and ages."

Angeles Arrien, Ph.D.,
Cultural anthropologist and author of *Working Together* and *The Four-Fold Way*

"My work with WMFDP has been some of the most interesting and informative of my entire professional career. The opportunity to learn and understand who I am as a white male, and all that entails both positive and negative, will help me interact more effectively with everyone."

David Ratcliffe
CEO
Southern Company

TESTIMONIALS

"This field guide offers a nonthreatening, enlightening challenge to action that gives white men, white women, and people of color the keys to creating more inclusive, satisfying and effective relationships across lines of difference. Blame, guilt and defensiveness are not part of this process. Clear information, guidelines and examples for real change are. This is a powerful addition to the resources for healthy, practical and effective diversity management."

Anita Rowe
Partner in Gardenswartz & Rowe and coauthor, *Managing Diversity: A Complete Desk Reference and Planning Guide*

CONTENTS

ACKNOWLEDGMENTS

Many people helped us in the creation of this field guide. Foremost we thank our clients, whose partnership has helped us shape and evolve our ideas. Our appreciation also goes to our associates, who share our passion, support our ongoing growth and help us proudly serve our clients. Special thanks to our business partner Tim McNichol who challenged and supported the evolution of our work. Thanks also to Jim Barber, Mike Kennedy, and Mark Chesler for reviewing this text and providing valuable feedback.

INTRODUCTION TO THE WMFDP FIELD GUIDE SERIES

White Men as Full Diversity Partners® (WMFDP, LLC) is a company driven by a desire to change the way diversity is practiced in the United States. We believe that building effective diversity partnerships creates critical leadership skills that have often been absent from most organizations' leadership development and diversity initiatives. We believe diversity partnerships leverage leadership skills and can be developed throughout an organization.

We are pursuing three goals in the establishment of diversity partnerships and inclusive organizations:

1] The first goal is the automatic inclusion of white men and their diversity rather than including everyone else but white men.

2] The second is the inclusion of work that women and men of color, and white women are invited to do to examine how their assumptions, interactions, and experiences influence their diversity partnerships with white men as well as their interactions with each other.

3] The third is the ability of leaders to see and act on the symbiotic relationship between leadership skill development and the creation of diversity partnerships. Linking leadership and diversity partnerships on a daily basis can transform mindsets and build skills. The results are courageous actions that benefit people and the goals of their organizations.

It doesn't matter to us what position you hold. What does matter is that all of us have work to do and a role to play in changing the way diversity is practiced and valued.

This field guide is a companion to another guide for white men, and a third field guide for white women, and men and women of color. These field guides outline the work each group needs to do to create breakthrough diversity partnerships. This guide was written to support you. In order to benefit, you will need to take action: read, reflect on the questions, experiment with the activities, and apply the insights to your work and life. Use this guide to increase your understanding of diversity, your leadership ability, and your diversity partnership skills. Your actions today and tomorrow are what count.

The partners and associates of WMFDP, LLC are grateful for our clients' courageous actions and persistence in doing the work that creates diversity partnerships and makes inclusive organizations a reality.

WHO SHOULD USE THIS FIELD GUIDE?

This field guide focuses on the practice and refinement of diversity partnership skills. It is written in a conversational tone and speaks directly to you the reader. Anyone who wants to learn more about partnerships and what it takes to build and sustain them can use and benefit from this field guide. Specifically, the guide is intended for:

- Business leaders and managers
- Diversity councils and employee networks
- Individuals and groups in for-profit and non-profit organizations
- Professors and their students

How to Use This Field Guide

This is a "take-action" field guide. It is designed for you to use interactively – at work, in your community and your personal life. No field guide works in the same way for any two people, so we have included a variety of ways to look at the topics explored in the field guide.

Historically, white women and people of color have done almost all of the work of educating white men on diversity issues. Transforming this dynamic – such that white men, white women, and women and men of color partner together effectively – is not effortless, but it is possible. Pursuing diversity partnership work requires new ways of thinking and new behaviors. All of the field guides were written to help you do the work; the choice is yours.

The first half of this field guide introduces tips, skill descriptions and reflective questions to help you apply the skills described.

The second section provides activities to further develop these skills. Some of the activities can be done individually, while others are suggested for group work. Work with each tip, or strategy, and use the field guide to push yourself further out onto your learning edge.

While these guides primarily address issues related to race and gender, many of the tips and questions are applicable to other kinds of difference; for example, sexual orientation, age and economic background. These diversity partnerships are also key to organizational health and business success.

Some helpful suggestions when using this field guide:

1] The intent of the field guide is to help you become more conscious and competent in the development and application of diversity partnership skills. It takes perseverance and practice. Don't expect perfection or immediate results.

2] Work alone and with others. Find ways to work with colleagues and/or friends. This work is about partnership and reflection. You might begin with solo reflection by answering questions you find in the field guide. Your next step might be to ask a colleague or friend to work with you. Have them act as a coach or mentor, someone to talk through how you are putting into action the tip or skill you chose.

3] Don't attempt to read through the field guide cover to cover. Take it one small chunk at a time. Read through each tip and work the one that appeals to you the most. Work with one reflective question at a time.

4] Take notes. Notice what is easy and makes sense and where you become confused and/or resistant. Use your coach to talk through those spots and seek learning that brings *immediate* relevancy to your diversity partnership efforts at work.

5] Acknowledge and celebrate each small step forward in strengthening your partnership skills practice. If you feel stuck in one spot, move onto another tip or reflective question.

6] This field guide is an entry into a variety of partnership strategies, not an exhaustive list. Approach the study of diversity partnership the way an anthropologist would go on a dig. Look at things from different angles. Be curious. Ask questions. Write your own reflective questions. Suspend judgment.

As you deepen your practice of diversity partnership we invite you to tell us what you are learning. Share reflective questions that you created by using this field guide. Your insights will help direct subsequent revisions of the guide. Email your comments and additions to **fieldguides@wmfdp.com**

Based on our experiences with a wide range of clients, if you commit to this skill-building adventure, you'll discover more choices in how you relate to and interact with others. You will become more aware of how you are developing and using your skills and resources in new ways. You will also be more equipped to use them in creating effective and satisfying partnerships built on shared understanding, whether at work or at home.

COURAGE

WHAT THIS SKILL LOOKS LIKE:

- I know the principles most dear to me. I stand by them.

- I may still be afraid, but I choose to function in spite of my fear, the risks involved, and any of my own discomfort.

- I am willing at times to say "I don't know" and join with others in searching for answers.

- I am able to take risks in speaking my truth and acting to create change.

The word courage literally means to "stand by one's core." Acting on courageous decisions requires knowing one's own core, the essence of one's principles and character. Courageous leadership is truly leadership from the inside out.

As a leader, the courage you demonstrate lets others know where you stand, whether you are trustworthy, and whether others would like to join you. Courage helps you maintain momentum in the face of uncertainty.

Tenacity and risk-taking historically helped European white men travel against great odds to America, and these qualities continue today as threads of American white male culture. Combining these with other cultural threads such as rugged individualism, head over heart, and the quiet determination signified in the phrase "run silent, run deep" creates a blend of courage that has white men "going it alone" and pursuing success where logic rules.

Leadership can be enhanced when courage-backed action is expanded beyond the world of certainty and logic into connecting with our hearts. Leading courageously from the heart enables us to build deeper, more significant partnerships with others.

REFLECTIVE QUESTIONS:

1] What key principles do I live by? What is the essence of my character? How do I demonstrate these in my leadership?

_____

_____

_____

_____

_____

_____

_____

_____

_____

_____

_____

2] Where in my life have I said difficult things to others? How did it affect the partnership? How did it expand and/or limit my influence on others?

_____

_____

_____

_____

_____

_____

_____

_____

_____

_____

_____

_____

3] Where in my life have I shown the most courage? What does that experience tell me about how to bring more of my courage to effective diversity partnerships and to my leadership practice?

_____

_____

_____

_____

_____

_____

_____

4] What have I wanted to tell a partner that I have chosen not to say, and why? If I had said it, what do I imagine might have happened to that partnership?

_____

_____

_____

_____

_____

_____

_____

5] When do I find myself silent? What is the effect of that silence on my partnerships?

_____

_____

_____

_____

_____

_____

_____

INTEGRATING HEAD AND HEART

WHAT THIS SKILL LOOKS LIKE:

- I value both my head and my heart.

- My intelligence is an important source of my leadership strength. I balance intellect with emotional maturity and the ability to empathize and connect with others.

- I know when and how to show vulnerability in a way that creates openness and authentic connection.

- I also know my own blind spots and growing edges. I recognize how my leadership presence affects others' performance.

The Chinese-language symbol for consensus literally means "the head and heart come together and speak with one voice." In contrast, American white male culture has emphasized rationality as the single source of truth and the primary key to success. Leaders fully grounded in both head and heart can access more of their internal resources and successfully lead more kinds of people; they are more powerful than those who attempt to lead with intellect alone.

REFLECTIVE QUESTIONS:

1] What examples do I have of people who use both their heads and their hearts at work? What do I observe and experience that tells me they are accessing head and heart? How does knowing this about them affect my willingness to partner with them? What skills might I develop in order to use similar traits?

_____

_____

_____

_____

_____

_____

_____

REFLECTIVE QUESTIONS *Continued*

2] What parts of myself might I hide from others that make my work life more difficult than it needs to be?

_____

_____

_____

_____

_____

_____

_____

_____

_____

_____

3] Where have I witnessed other people being vulnerable? In what ways was this a strength?

_____

_____

_____

_____

_____

_____

_____

_____

_____

_____

_____

4] How might what I learned growing up about the value or non-value of expressing either head or heart be helping or hindering my ability to partner today?

_____

_____

_____

_____

_____

_____

_____

_____

_____

_____

_____

_____

_____

_____

_____

_____

_____

_____

_____

_____

_____

_____

_____

_____

This skill can also be enhanced by doing activity #1 in the activity session.

LISTENING

WHAT THIS SKILL LOOKS LIKE:

- I can fully hear others whose perspectives are different from mine.

- I can accept their viewpoints as valid.

- If necessary, I can repeat back the essence of their perspectives so they know that I grasp their views. This creates shared understanding; it does not mean I agree with their perspectives.

- I am able to listen to others' perspectives without interrupting to defend my perspective.

- I know how to acknowledge others' ideas as a way to broaden my point of view.

- I can step out of a debate mode of conversation when the goal is to have a conversation for learning.

T he word "respect" literally means "the willingness to look again." I give others a second look rather than lock myself into a quick judgment.

As a leader, this second look allows me to know how others experience a given situation, develops my own empathy and compassion, and builds relationships that maximize opportunity for learning and partnership.

Woven through white male culture in America is a value placed on arguing and winning debates, which emphasizes logic. Emotion is usually limited to expressions of anger, which for men may be viewed as a sign of strong determined leadership. I learned that it is more important to prove my point and think of a rebuttal than to truly listen to understand others. As a result, conversations end with a winner, a loser, and little shared understanding. Leaders can miss important wisdom if they assume everyone around the table contributes by argument and logic.

When I add "listening fully" to my toolkit, I complement the advocacy skills I already have with inquiry skills. My advocacy skills give me voice. My inquiry skills help me learn collaboratively with others. Both are critical for leadership success. I learn to see the world through others' eyes. My vision of the world gets broader.

REFLECTIVE QUESTIONS:

1] What will help me stay open to others' realities to understand them more fully,
   rather than judge them from my frame of reference?

_____

_____

_____

_____

_____

_____

2] What causes me to stop listening to others? If I stop listening, where does
   my attention go? What is the effect of my attention shift?

_____

_____

_____

_____

_____

_____

3] How do/can I practice staying present, focused, and respectful of others'
   perspectives in the face of their displays of emotion? Where have I seen someone
   be able to display emotion and rationality simultaneously?

_____

_____

_____

_____

_____

_____

_____

4] How do I judge the use of emotion at work? What am I likely to say about people who display emotion at work? How might what I say affect their credibility?

_____

_____

_____

_____

_____

_____

_____

_____

_____

_____

_____

_____

5] What opportunities for leadership development and action do my answers offer me?

_____

_____

_____

_____

_____

_____

_____

_____

_____

_____

_____

_____

BALANCING KEY PARADOXES

WHAT THIS SKILL LOOKS LIKE:

- I know that successful leadership requires me to satisfy many contradictory needs and goals.

- These elements are interdependent; to satisfy one I must address the others.

- I am most successful when I try to balance these opposites.

- I recognize that some of my leadership challenges aren't really problems to solve but ongoing paradoxes to manage.

G iven the emphasis on rationality in white male culture, white men and others immersed in this culture do not naturally subscribe to the notion that opposing needs or goals should be simultaneously pursued. This *either/or* mindset can lead us to attempt to solve problems with a single solution. Either/or problem solving can exacerbate complex problems. Leadership is enhanced by looking at the relationship between problems that seem opposing or unrelated.

EXAMPLES OF PARADOXES TO BALANCE INCLUDE:

INDIVIDUALLY: *talking* and *listening, being direct* and *being nice, being appreciative* and *being critical, etc.*

IN A TEAM: *focusing on the work* and *focusing on the team's own process, spending time planning* and *spending time doing the work, being clear with a predetermined plan* and *being flexible with what emerges, etc.*

ORGANIZATIONALLY: *organizing by product or service* and *organizing by function, valuing productivity* and *quality, having uniform rules* and *unit autonomy.*

REFLECTIVE QUESTIONS:

1] How does my language about issues such as diversity management set up *either/or* or *both/and* propositions? What is the effect of *either/or* and *both/and* on my thinking, my decisions, my performance, and my organization?

_____

_____

_____

_____

_____

_____

_____

_____

_____

2] How is my leadership balanced in terms of fully challenging AND supporting others as well as being both critical AND appreciative?

_____

_____

_____

_____

_____

_____

_____

_____

_____

3] Where do I find myself in relation to complexity as discussed in the following quote?

"I would not give a fig for the simplicity this side of complexity, but I would give my life for the simplicity on the other side of complexity."
Oliver Wendell Holmes

_____

_____

_____

_____

_____

_____

_____

_____

_____

_____

_____

_____

_____

_____

_____

_____

_____

_____

_____

_____

_____

_____

This skill can also be enhanced by doing activity #2 in the activity session.

LEVERAGING AMBIGUITY AND TURBULENCE

WHAT THIS SKILL LOOKS LIKE:

- I accept complexity and ambiguity as constant reality in much of the world. Being open to paradoxes gives me a deeper perspective.

- Life is both simple and complex; this is one of many paradoxes I embrace.

- I police my own need to oversimplify the world as a way to maintain blindness to things that don't fit my worldview.

- I recognize when I am falling into *either/or* thinking and can extend my view to include *both/and* thinking.

- I have learned to extend patience to myself and others.

- I understand that ambiguity and change create an atmosphere of turbulence. Leadership requires that I simultaneously manage my own and others' resistance to this turbulence *and* use it as an opportunity to remove both real and perceived barriers to change.

either/or thinking assumes there is a right and wrong, with little gray area in between. The Calvinistic roots of white male culture hold a predisposition to *either/or* thinking. Within these roots is a very low tolerance for uncertainty. Today's world, though, is more complex. Leadership today requires more skill in managing ambiguity and working in the midst of the confusion that results when there are many sides to an issue. Leadership is strengthened by developing the ability to leverage ambiguity and turbulence.

REFLECTIVE QUESTIONS:

1] What helps me keep focused on things I can't measure or be certain of?

_____

_____

_____

_____

_____

_____

_____

_____

_____

2] How does my need for certainty mask the complexity inherent in diversity issues?

_____

_____

_____

_____

_____

_____

_____

_____

_____

_____

_____

3] What are common ways I respond to ambiguity and confusion? What helps me operate effectively in environments of uncertainty?

_____

_____

_____

_____

_____

_____

_____

_____

_____

_____

_____

_____

_____

4] What are some of the contradictory demands placed on my life, and how do I manage the tension? How does this tension strengthen me as a leader and/or individual contributor?

_____

_____

_____

_____

_____

_____

_____

_____

_____

_____

5] What allows me to be more comfortable managing the uncertainty and turbulence of a changing external business environment and often less comfortable managing the turbulence and uncertainty related to issues of diversity? Why is one easier than the other?

_____

_____

_____

_____

_____

_____

_____

_____

_____

_____

This skill can also be enhanced by doing activity #3 in the activity session.

MANAGING DIFFICULT CONVERSATIONS

WHAT THIS SKILL LOOKS LIKE:

- I initiate and engage in direct, honest and timely conversations, without blame, in order to maximize partnership and business success.

- I acknowledge immediately when something is not working and stop doing it.

- In listening to others, I recognize when I am observing behavior and when I am adding my own interpretation to that behavior.

- I can then fully choose when to give clear feedback and when to share my own perspective.

- I avoid attributing negative intentions to others and monitor my own intentions while communicating.

- I don't collude with my own stereotypes about other people.

Many factors influence whether people communicate directly or not. American white male culture tends to value direct communication, although men's emotional sharing may be limited to anger. Other feelings of confusion, uncertainty, fear, or the sadness behind anger will likely not be shared. Emphasis on rationality and advocacy, rather than inquiry, may lead difficult conversations to follow the format of a debate, with the intention of having a winner and a loser. Often the complexity of a conflict is oversimplified by the search for a "right" and a "wrong" perspective.

In contrast, where the emphasis is on inquiry, a learning conversation takes place with a goal of understanding. Leadership is enhanced by looking for the truth in each person's story. These stories can then be used to create a broader picture to get to the heart of conflicts without projecting negative intent, which blocks full understanding.

REFLECTIVE QUESTIONS:

1] When "being right" ceases to be a requirement, what are the potential effects on my ability to be an effective diversity partner?

_____

_____

_____

_____

_____

_____

_____

_____

_____

2] To what degree am I conscious of when I am observing behavior and when I am making interpretations or excuses for my own and others' behavior?

_____

_____

_____

_____

_____

_____

_____

_____

3] What options do I have in responding to someone else's anger? What might help me know whether what I experience as anger may in fact be another's attempt to express something else? Which of my own emotions am I comfortable expressing at work? How does that affect how I hear and respond to others' displays of emotion? How does my comfort level with the expression of emotion affect my ability to stay engaged in difficult conversations and/or in the partnership?

_____

_____

_____

_____

_____

_____

_____

_____

_____

_____

_____

_____

_____

4] Reflecting on my answers above, what do I need to do more of to enhance my leadership effectiveness? What do I need to do less of?

_____

_____

_____

_____

_____

_____

_____

_____

_____

_____

_____

_____

_____

_____

_____

_____

_____

_____

_____

_____

_____

_____

_____

_____

This skill can also be enhanced by doing activity #4 in the activity session.

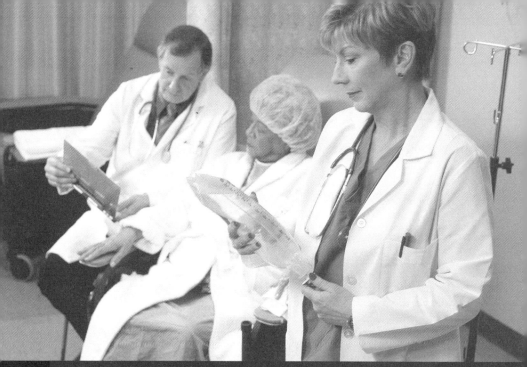

SEEING/THINKING SYSTEMICALLY

WHAT THIS SKILL LOOKS LIKE:

- I understand that I am part of many different social-identity groups and that this affects both my experience of the world and how others see me.

- I look beyond individual ways of knowing, to explore and make sense of patterns that I would not see if I looked at myself and others only as disconnected individuals.

- I know that culture is created in part by shared assumptions embedded in groups of people. I know these assumptions create dynamics of inclusion and exclusion.

- I continuously seek to understand and interrupt these dynamics in order to create a more equitable and just world.

The rugged individualism of American white male culture can lead to an overemphasis on seeing people as individuals, and an underemphasis on seeing systemic dynamics of group membership. Leadership competency is developed and/or strengthened by using both lenses: seeing people as individuals *and* recognizing the impact of their membership in many different groups on their experience. By understanding the complexities of these memberships, leaders can become sensitive to the possibility that others' realities are different from their own. Their view of the world broadens, as does their ability to influence the dynamics they previously did not see. Their previous view of the world wasn't necessarily wrong. More likely, it was incomplete.

Examples of social-identity groups include: race, gender, sexual orientation, age, religion, social class, education level, physical ability and size, mental ability, country of origin. All of these, and many others, provide a thread in the fabric of both who we are and how we experience the world.

REFLECTIVE QUESTIONS:

1] What group memberships are key to my colleagues? What don't I know or see about my colleague's day-to-day experiences that might be affecting our day-to-day partnership interactions? An example might help here: s/he was stopped on the way to work by a police officer for no reason s/he could see as legitimate. I was the first person s/he saw just after it happened.

_____

_____

_____

_____

_____

_____

_____

_____

_____

_____

_____

_____

_____

_____

_____

_____

_____

_____

_____

_____

_____

_____

_____

_____

2] Given what I've read about white male culture so far, where does this culture show up in my workplace and in how I work?

_____

_____

_____

_____

_____

_____

_____

_____

_____

_____

3] When someone says something or does something inappropriate and I do nothing, what effect do I have on the current situation and on future dynamics? Is my inaction more supportive of change or the status quo?

_____

_____

_____

_____

_____

_____

_____

_____

_____

_____

This skill can also be enhanced by doing activity #5 in the activity session.

BEING AN AGENT OF CHANGE

WHAT THIS SKILL LOOKS LIKE:

- I understand the common pathways of creating learning and change, both for individuals and organizations.

- I know how to respond to resistance to change and how to use myself as a leader/individual contributor to effectively support complex organizational change.

- My leadership is enhanced when I embrace the chaos that comes with change, and when I understand the feelings people experience during change.

- I demonstrate how to create inclusion, ownership and commitment while implementing change.

Western culture views change most often as a rational, linear process. Yet human beings are inherently non-rational, and change processes involving humans are usually nonlinear. Leaders who accept the existence of nonrational aspects of change in their organizations can learn to tap the expression of resistance and emotional turmoil as important fuel for driving organizational change.

REFLECTIVE QUESTIONS:

1] Which of my partnerships energize me as a leader and change agent?

_____

_____

_____

_____

_____

_____

_____

_____

_____

2] What have I learned are the most effective ways to respond to others' resistance to change?

_____

_____

_____

_____

_____

_____

_____

_____

_____

_____

3] In the midst of change, what makes me less effective in my partnerships with others, including other white men? My behaviors and actions? Their behaviors and actions?

_____

_____

_____

_____

_____

_____

_____

_____

_____

_____

_____

_____

_____

4] What do my partnerships teach me about effective change? What do my diversity partnerships teach me about implementation of effective change?

_____
_____
_____
_____
_____
_____
_____
_____
_____
_____
_____
_____
_____
_____
_____
_____
_____
_____
_____
_____
_____
_____
_____
_____
_____
_____

ACTIVITIES

ACTIVITY 1

HEAD AND HEART FORCE-FIELD ANALYSIS

ACTIVITY 2

FREEING ONESELF FROM A PARADOX TRAP

ACTIVITY 3

TRYING ON TURBULENCE

ACTIVITY 4

ANALYZING A DIFFICULT CONVERSATION

ACTIVITY 5

THE UNSPOKEN RULES

HEAD AND HEART FORCE-FIELD ANALYSIS

This is an individual activity. A group variation is described below.

How does your environment affect the degree to which you engage in life both from your head and your heart? Our lives include people, groups and organizations that influence this question. This activity offers a way to use the tool of force-field analysis to map these forces on your life.

Goal: To identify external influences in your life that lead you to live more in your head or more in your heart. Additionally, respond to the question of whether this head / heart balance is where you would like it to be.
Time Needed: 20 minutes.

STEPS:

1] In the diagram on this page, list along the lefthand column all the external forces you can identify that encourage you to connect and live from your heart.
The stronger the force, the bolder you can make the arrow under the listed force.

2] Now list in the righthand column all the external forces you can identify that encourage you to connect and live from your head. You may have identified the same force on both sides of the line.

FORCES ENCOURAGING HEART	FORCES ENCOURAGING HEAD

3] Now step back and notice the composite balance of forces pushing you in each direction. The following questions may help:

a. Collectively, which forces are strongest? Pushing downward to your heart or upward to your head?

_____

_____

_____

_____

_____

_____

_____

b. How does this affect your leadership effectiveness? Is your leadership style balanced, or are you overusing one strength at the expense of the other?

_____

_____

_____

_____

_____

_____

c. What shift would you like to make to improve your effectiveness?

_____

_____

_____

_____

_____

_____

_____

d. Looking at the forces, which ones might you change to support your desired goal? Note that in force-field analysis it is said that change can sometimes happen more easily by minimizing some of the "restraining forces" (those preventing you from reaching your goal) than by increasing your "driving forces" (that drive you toward your goal).

_____

_____

_____

_____

_____

_____

_____

_____

_____

_____

_____

_____

_____

_____

_____

_____

_____

_____

_____

_____

_____

_____

Variation: For a group setting: Do steps one and two alone. Then do the reflection in step three with a partner for 10-20 minutes. Afterward have a large-group discussion sharing insights from the exercise as well as identifying key forces that may be shared by multiple members of the group. How can the group support individuals moving in their preferred directions toward head or heart?

ACTIVITY 2

FREEING ONESELF FROM A PARADOX TRAP

This is an individual activity. A group variation is described below.

Paradoxes are difficult to conceptualize, accept and manage. If we don't manage key paradoxes in our lives, they will likely manage us. This activity offers a way to analyze your way around a paradox, and identify options to handle the paradox in a different way.

Goal: To analyze a paradox influencing your life, and to identify new ways to manage the paradox that result in increasing your effectiveness as a leader or individual contributor.
Time Needed: 20-30 minutes

STEPS:

1] Choose a paradox to analyze that is currently limiting your effectiveness. Paradoxes are often interdependent opposites. As leaders, if one side of a paradox is overused it can become a leadership weakness.

Example 1: Being more of a talker than a listener.

_____

_____

_____

_____

_____

_____

_____

_____

_____

_____

_____

_____

Example 2: Being more of a follower than a leader.

_____

_____

_____

_____

_____

_____

2] List: What keeps you on one side or the other of a paradox?

_____

_____

_____

_____

_____

_____

3] List: How would you be seen if you utilized both sides?

_____

_____

_____

_____

_____

_____

4] List: Why can't you tolerate being seen in this way? What might be motivating
your intolerance?

_____

_____

_____

_____

_____

5] Compare these three lists.

_____

_____

_____

_____

_____

_____

6] Choose one thing you might be able to practice that would allow you to tolerate the intolerable.

_____

_____

_____

_____

_____

_____

7] Identify what keeps you in *either/or*.

_____

_____

_____

_____

_____

8] What image keeps you in *either/or?*

_____

_____

_____

_____

_____

_____

9] What images move you into *both/and?*

_____

_____

_____

_____

_____

_____

_____

_____

_____

_____

10] How can you stretch to expand your leadership?

_____

_____

_____

_____

_____

_____

_____

_____

_____

_____

Variation: For a group setting: Individuals can do the above steps alone and
then share them with a partner. This can be followed by a large-group discussion
of insights gained from doing the exercise. Some individuals may be willing to
share their paradox as examples.

ACTIVITY 3

TRYING ON TURBULENCE

This activity is done with a partner. Parts of it can also be done alone.

Most of the time we think of turbulence as something to cope with and endure. Few of us look to turbulence as our teacher. This activity experiments with leveraging turbulence to become more effective leaders.

Goal: To discover ways to use turbulence and its effects as a way to sharpen your leadership effectiveness.
Time Needed: 75 minutes (steps 1-3)

STEPS:

1] Reflect alone for five minutes on the following question: Where does turbulence and unpredictability show up most in your life?

_____

_____

_____

_____

_____

_____

_____

_____

_____

2] Pair up with another individual and use the following questions to interview each other for approximately 20 minutes each. When interviewing, play the role of a curious investigator, taking notes on key insights.

Describe a time when there was a high level of turbulence in your life and you not only managed to navigate it but you thrived on it. You were able to function at extraordinary levels despite the turbulence and uncertainty in your work and/or life.

What about your performance was extraordinary?

_____

_____

_____

_____

_____

_____

What made exceptional execution possible?

_____

_____

_____

_____

_____

_____

What skills and behaviors helped with the success of this moment?

_____

_____

_____

_____

_____

_____

What did you do to contribute to thriving on turbulence?

_____

_____

_____

_____

_____

_____

3] Now identify a specific trigger that moved you *away* from turbulence recently in your work or home life. Discuss with your partner how you can apply insights from your interview about successfully engaging turbulence in the past to change how you react now to this trigger. Take about 15 minutes each.

4] Now actually experiment with this trigger over time—at a staff meeting, with a person, etc. Take notes on what you learn.

_____

_____

_____

_____

_____

_____

_____

_____

_____

_____

_____

_____

_____

_____

_____

_____

_____

5] Report back to your interview partner; let the person know that day what you tried and what learning occurred. Acknowledge to each other the work you have done and talk about any needs for skill development you've discovered.

ANALYZING A DIFFICULT CONVERSATION

This is an individual activity. A group variation is described below.

Goal: To gain insight into ways to both think differently and approach
a conflict differently.
Time Needed: 30-40 minutes

STEPS:
A. Reflect on a recent or current conflict or difficult conversation either at work
   or at home. The following section presents the five key points adapted from the
   book *Difficult Conversations* (see Suggested Reading) and offers reflective questions
   for each point. Write notes under each question as you reflect on a recent
   or current conflict.

1] The problem is often the difference between two stories. Neither story is the
   right one, or the truth.
   What is the other person's story?

_____

_____

_____

_____

_____

_____

_____

_____

   What are the main differences between my story and their story?

_____

_____

_____

_____

_____

_____

2] We assume negative intent or negative character.
In their words, what were their actual intentions?

_____

_____

_____

_____

_____

_____

3] Move from assigning blame to mapping out the contributions of each person.
What is my contribution to the conflict?

_____

_____

_____

_____

_____

_____

What is their contribution to the conflict?

_____

_____

_____

_____

_____

4] Acknowledge and express our feelings.
What feelings underlie my attributions and judgments? Have I shared my feelings?

_____

_____

_____

_____

What feelings underlie their attributions and judgments?
Have they shared their feelings?

_____

_____

_____

_____

_____

_____

_____

_____

5] Recognize that conflict can be a threat to our sense of who we are.
What identity issues surface for me? How does what happened threaten my identity?

_____

_____

_____

_____

_____

_____

_____

_____

What identity issues surface for them?
How does what happened threaten their identity?

_____

_____

_____

_____

_____

_____

_____

_____

B. What new insights have emerged from your reflections above? What new insights
    do you have about this conflict and about difficult conversations in general?

_____

_____

_____

_____

_____

_____

_____

_____

_____

Variation: For a group setting: step A can be done individually in 15-20 minutes.
Step B can be shared either in pairs or as a whole group in 15-20 minutes. If your
group is a team you may want to consider taking 20-40 minutes for step C, below.

C. Discuss these questions as a team: How might we as a team utilize the five points
    above to create guidelines on how to discuss difficult matters with each other?
    What principles do we want to agree on to guide how we resolve conflict in our
    team? How can we support each other in continuing to develop our skills at
    engaging in healthy conflict for the purpose of building creativity and working
    through the natural challenges of team high-performance?

_____

_____

_____

_____

_____

_____

_____

_____

_____

_____

_____

THE UNSPOKEN RULES

This activity can be done either individually or as a group.

Assumptions held by founders and core members of organizations are often taken for granted. These cultural elements affect everyone, sometimes in both positive and negative ways. These often invisible assumptions can contribute to both organizational effectiveness and ineffectiveness. Being able to decipher assumptions embedded in the fabric of an organization's culture requires the leadership skill of thinking systemically.

Goal: To identify aspects of organizational culture and its effect on organizations.
Time Needed: 1 hour

STEPS:

1] List the attributes of your organization's culture. What are the spoken rules? What are the often unspoken rules? Sometimes they can be recognized when someone receives penalties for violating them. What are new people taught about how things are done?

_____

_____

_____

_____

_____

_____

_____

_____

_____

_____

_____

_____

2] Rank these attributes from most visible to least visible.

_____

_____

_____

_____

_____

_____

_____

_____

_____

_____

_____

3] Rank these attributes from most valued to least valued.

_____

_____

_____

_____

_____

_____

_____

_____

_____

_____

_____

4] Brainstorm the upsides and downsides for each rule.

_____

_____

_____

_____

_____

_____

_____

_____

_____

_____

_____

_____

5] Explore how each rule affects daily interactions and organizational culture.

_____

_____

_____

_____

_____

_____

_____

_____

_____

_____

_____

_____

6] Examine what the costs are to people in the organization.

_____

_____

_____

_____

_____

_____

_____

_____

_____

_____

_____

7] Consider and list ways to manage those costs.

_____

_____

_____

_____

_____

_____

_____

_____

_____

_____

_____

APPENDICES

KEY CONCEPTS

European-American or American White Male Culture

Culture describes shared values and beliefs of a group. U.S. American white male culture is interesting in that it can be seen and described by those who are not members of the culture, yet for many white men the characteristics they share with other white men are most often invisible. This stems in part from the fact that most white men rarely have to step out of their culture, while many white women and people of color learn to be bi-cultural, often moving in and out of white male culture on a daily basis. The paradox is that in order for one to best understand one's culture, one has to leave it.

The shared characteristics of white men in the United States determine, in large part, how things get done and the norms of interaction, both business and personal. Within a culture, individuals will vary in their knowledge, acceptance and support of the culture. Some won't know they are members of a group with a distinct culture. There are six themes of the U.S. white male culture we engage in our work:

- Rugged individualism
- Low tolerance for uncertainty and ambiguity
- Focus on action over reflection (doing over being)
- Rationality over emotion (head over heart)
- Time as linear and future focused
- Status and rank over connection

The cultural literature often refers to the above characteristics as "American Culture" while at the same time identifying African American, Asian American and other ethnic subcultures of the U.S. as something else. The white male facet of what is simply described as American Culture often goes unspoken and remains invisible.

Since most organizations and institutions in the U.S. are based on white male cultural values such as those listed above, all of us — white men, white women, and people of color — have learned to operate in this culture.

A brief note about the words we use. Technically speaking the term European-American refers more to ethnicity and region of origin, while the terms white and male refer more to race and gender, respectively. We have chosen to describe the above culture more often as white male culture in the U.S. in part because we have found many white men tend to more easily identify themselves as white male than European-American. Please use the term you most prefer.

Partnership and Partnership Culture
Partner: A person associated with another or member of a business partnership.

Have you ever felt like a child at work? Have you ever wondered why your manager thought you needed to be protected from what everyone knew was coming (downsizing, a merger, plant closings, a new CEO, etc.)? When you have that feeling or are asking similar questions, you are probably responding to the parental nature of organizations. Most organizations are hierarchical and depend on predictability, and command and control, to meet business goals. Another way to think about the parental nature of organizations is to view them as patriarchal – or "father knows best." Patriarchy is different than building a diversity partnership culture in our organizations. Peter Block dedicates Chapter Two of his 1993 book, *Stewardship*, to partnership as an alternative to patriarchy. We believe that diversity partnerships are on the cutting edge of changing organizations. Block describes partnership as having four requirements that need to be demonstrated for real partnership to develop. His requirements fit the intention of White Men As Full Diversity Partners®' diversity partnership work.

Block's four requirements for real partnership include:
- Exchange of purpose – "Purpose gets defined through dialogue." (Block, 1993 p. 29)
- Right to say no – "If we cannot say no, then saying yes has no meaning." (p. 30)
- Joint accountability – Each person is responsible for outcomes and the current situation. "If people in organizations want the freedom partnership offers, the price of that freedom is to take personal accountability for the success and failure of our unit and our community." (p. 30)
- Absolute honesty – It's essential for partnership. (p. 30)

Crutch-Free Diversity Partnership Framework
- Our respective roles are clear and we understand them rather than assuming what we each mean. I ask before assuming I know.

- We agree on how we will engage conflict.

- We actively apply and live in the key paradoxes. Individually, we take time to find out whether our perspectives match, or not. We look at how each of us uses the paradoxes – how we demonstrate them in our behavior.

- We use frequent direct feedback about what works in the partnership and what doesn't work. We listen to understand. We talk about how the contributions we make to our partnership affect our commitment to our work and each other.

- We acknowledge the steps we've taken to support and challenge each other. We recognize that our diversity partners may have very different views and understandings of the issues we are facing together. We acknowledge that our frames of reference have been affected by differences of gender, race, class, sexual orientation, experience, etc. It's our job to understand each other's world views and their influence on how we work together.

- We show respect for each other in the moment…when it counts. Some of these moments will occur when our partner is not present. These will be opportunities we can use to demonstrate respect for our partner and our partnership.

- We attend to a broken trust between us, rather than assume that our partnership is a lost cause. "Once broken, never regained," is unacceptable as our first response. Tears in the fabric of our partnership are used to test our commitment, demonstrate tenacity and build skill. We refuse to hold on to misunderstandings. We do that by scheduling time to air and resolve misunderstandings.

Paradox

The American Heritage Dictionary of the English Language defines paradox as a seemingly contradictory statement that may nonetheless be true. Another of its definitions suggests that paradox can and does live in an individual, group, situation or action that exhibits inexplicable or contradictory aspects.

Contradictions often contain conflict, particularly when the contradictions co-exist at the same time in the same individual, group and/or situation. Diversity partnership is a hotbed of paradox. We offer four that show up repeatedly in diversity partnership work that require conscious attention and skill building. Diversity partners build skill at living with paradox and conflict. Kenwyn K. Smith and David N. Berg describe paradox in detail in their book, *Paradoxes of Group Life*.

Paradox #1 – Individual/Group:

White men are *both* individuals *and* members of the white male group. When white men acknowledge their membership in the white male group, they do not give up their individuality.

Example:
"Don't lump me in with other white guys. Maybe I'm different."
"I've never thought of myself as being a member of a white male group, and I am."

Paradox *Continued*

Paradox #2 – Difference/Sameness

A deeper picture of diversity requires both a focus on difference *and* sameness, diversity *and* commonality. Each can only be defined in terms of the other. For example, being color-conscious *and* color-blind simultaneously.

Example:
"I treat everyone the same. I don't see color."
"I want my coworkers to see my color. It's an important part of me."

Paradox #3 – Support/Challenge

Breakthrough learning is created by diversity partners who support *and* challenge each other. Partners do not choose one or the other side of this or any paradox. Both sides are necessary in effective results-focused diversity partnerships.

Example:
"We need to be patient and understanding here…let people come along at their own pace."
"That behavior is wrong and it must change."

Paradox #4 – No Fault/Responsibility:

It is not my fault *and* I am responsible. Often white men feel they are being asked to carry the personal burden of the historical mistreatment of other groups. It is not our fault and we are vital parts of the dialogue needed to create more equitable systems for everyone, including white men.

Example:
"I didn't create this situation…and I can and will look at my responsibility for keeping it in place."

Difficult Conversations

A difficult conversation is any conversation you find hard to initiate, participate in and complete. Difficult conversations require preparation. The ability to engage in difficult conversations is a key concept of diversity partnership work.*

Difficult conversations have three parts:

1. **Content:** What is it you want to talk about? What are your intentions for discussing it?

2. **Feelings:** What are you feeling as you prepare for the conversation? It does little good to attempt to hide or bury your feelings.

3. **The identity conversation:** How does this situation threaten our sense of who we are?

Preparation:

- Uncover your assumptions and *intentions* before you schedule time for the conversation.

- Don't assume you know your partner's intentions. You don't.

- Difficult conversations require risk-taking; take some.

*This material has been adapted from the book *Difficult Conversations*.

GLOSSARY

Systemic Privilege/Advantage
Systemic privilege is the unspoken and unacknowledged benefits that come to a person through no virtue of their own but are made to look normal and available to any person who wants them. These benefits are often invisible to those who receive them and clearly visible to those who don't.

Classism
Classism is prejudice and/or discrimination, either personal or institutional, against people because of their real or perceived economic status or background. *(http://cluh2.tripod.com/definitions.html#classism)*

Collusion
Collusion is the often unconscious actions that reinforce/support the status quo that benefit some at the expense of others. Collusion can be conscious or unconscious, active or passive.

Heterosexism
Heterosexism is action taken to limit people's rights and privileges or access to them, based on the conscious or unconscious belief or opinion that heterosexuality is the normal and right expression of sexuality and any other expression is abnormal and wrong. The privileges and rights that are denied can be legislative, public and familial.

Fluid Identity
Fluid Identity is the concept that identity is not rigid but can and does change. This idea is often used in terms of gender, sexuality, and race, as well as other factors of identity. This concept is fundamentally contrary to binary systems. A person who feels her/his identity is fluid often believes that rigid categories are oppressive and incapable of accurately describing her/his experience and identities. *(http://cluh2.tripod.com/)*

Homophobia
Homophobia is the fear or hatred of gays, lesbians, or queer-identified people in general. It can be manifested as an intense dislike or rejection of such people, or violent actions against them. *(http://cluh2.tripod.com/definitions.html)*
See the definition of Heterosexism, above.

Sex Reassignment Surgery (SRS)

SRS is the surgical procedure to modify one's primary sexual characteristics (genitalia) from those of one sex to those of the opposite sex. SRS may also include secondary surgery such as breast augmentation or reduction and/or removing the Adam's apple. *(http://www.tg2tg.org/forums/lifestyles)*

SOFFA

A SOFFA is a Significant Other, Friend, Family, or Ally of a transsexual, transgender, inter-sex or other gender-variant person. *(http://www.virtualcity.com/)*

Transgender (TG)

Transgender is a more recently adopted umbrella term that includes all persons who engage in cross-gender activities or lifestyles regardless of motivation or sexual orientation. *(http://www.tg2tg.org/forums/lifestyles)*

Transsexual* (TS)

Transsexual describes an individual whose gender identity is the opposite of his or her physical sex. Typically such individuals desire modification of their physical body (i.e., SRS) to match their gender identity, and derive no "thrill," erotic or otherwise, from merely wearing the clothing associated with the opposite biological gender. *(http://www.tg2tg.org/forums/lifestyles)*

* Transsexual may also be spelled transexual, depending on country of origin. *(http://pages.sbcglobal.net/texasrat/page9.html)*

White Guilt

White guilt is a frequent response of white people to learning about white privilege. White guilt makes white individuals feel shameful about the history of oppression of people of color and the role white persons have played in perpetuating that system, as well as their individual complicity with that system. *(http://cluh2.tripod.com/definitions.html)*

SUGGESTED READING:

Arrien, Angeles. *The Four-Fold Way: Walking the Paths of the Warrior, Teacher, Healer, and Visionary.* HarperSanFrancisco: 1993. ISBN: 0-06-250059-7

Bilodeau, M.S., Lorrainne. *The Anger Workbook.* MIF Books: 1992. ISBN: 1-56731-202-0

Block, Peter. *Stewardship.* Berrett Koehler: 1993. ISBN: 1-881052-28-1

Bridges, William. *Managing Transitions, Making The Most of Change.* Addison Wesley: 1991. ISBN: 0-201-55073-3

Cashman, Kevin. *Leadership from the Inside Out.* Executive Excellence Publishing: 1998. ISBN: 1-890009-29-6

Dana, Daniel, Ph.D, *Managing Differences: How to Build Better Relationships at Work and Home.* MTI Publications: 1997. ISBN: 0-9621534-3-5

Goleman, Daniel, Richard Boyatzis, and Annie McKee. *Primal Leadership: Realizing The Power Of Emotional Intelligence.* Harvard Business School Press: 2002. ISBN:1-57851-486-X

Johnson, Barry. *Polarity Management: Identifying and Managing Unsolvable Problems.* Human Resource Development Press: 1992. ISBN: 0-87425-176-1

Lukeman, Alex and Gayle. *Beyond Blame: Reclaiming The Power You Give To Others.* North Star Publications: 1997. ISBN: 1-880823-14-4

Maurer, Rick. *Feedback Toolkit: 16 Tools for Better Communication in the Workplace.* Productivity Press: 1994. ISBN:1-56327-056-0

McGraw, Phillip C., Ph.D. *Life Strategies: Doing What Works, Doing What Matters.* Hyperion: 1999. ISBN: 0-7868-8459-2

Pfeffer, Jeffrey. *Managing with Power: Politics and Influence in Organizations.* Harvard Business School Press: 1992. ISBN: 0-87584-314-X

Scott, Susan. *Fierce Conversations: Achieving Success at Work & in Life, One Conversation at a Time.* Berkley Books: 2002. ISBN: 0-425-19337-3

Stone, Douglas, Bruce Patton and Sheila Heen. *Difficult Conversations: How to Discuss What Matters Most.* Penguin Books: 2000. ISBN: 0-14-028852 X

Takaki, Ronald. *From Different Shores: Perspectives on Race and Ethnicity in America.* Second Edition. Oxford University Press: 1994. ISBN: 0-19-508368-7

Takaki, Ronald. *A Different Mirror: A History of Multicultural America*, 1993. ISBN: 0-316-83111-5

Wheatley, Margaret, J. *Leadership and the New Science: Discovering Order in a Chaotic World.* Berrett-Koehler Publishers: 1999. ISBN: 1-57675-055-8

Whyte, David. *The Heart Aroused: Poetry and the Preservation of the Soul in Corporate America.* Revised Edition. Doubleday: 2002. ISBN 0-385-48418-6

Wylie, Pete, Dr., and Dr. Mardy Grothe. *Can This Partnership Be Saved? Improving (or Salvaging) Your Key Business Relationships.* Upstart Publishing Company, Inc.: 1993. ISBN: 0-936894-42-3

www.wmfdp.com
See the Online Resources page.

Diversity Partnership Tips for White Men: A Skills Building Field Guide

By Bill Proudman, Michael Welp, Jo Ann Morris

At last, a book that puts the invisible partners of diversity – white men – in the spotlight. This paradigm-busting field guide invites white men to step out of the shadows and fully join their organizations' diversity efforts. Because, contrary to popular belief, their engagement is critical to the success of any serious diversity initiative. Only when white men form vital partnerships with other white men, white women and people of color can organizations move from mere pro forma head count increases to a genuinely new, inclusive culture. Part of the challenge is understanding where white men are coming from. You'll learn what white male culture is, and how it affects the white man's business success. And you may be surprised to find out that despite their dominant position, white men are often overtly excluded from mainstream diversity efforts. That's not a good thing, because there are powerful reasons why white men should care about – and invest in – diversity initiatives (hint: the stakes are much higher than most white men realize). Choosing to get involved in diversity actually helps white men build leadership skills; we'll show you how. Plus, we outline new ways to smash old barriers so white men can partner more effectively with others.

$15.95 ISBN 0-9754192-1-8

order books at www.wmfdp.com

Diversity Partnership Tips for White Women and People of Color to Engage White Men: A Skills Building Field Guide

By Jo Ann Morris, Bill Proudman, Michael Welp

Open this book, open your mind, and climb out of your box. This field guide tackles workplace diversity with startling candor and delivers refreshingly practical solutions for individuals and groups. You'll encounter provocative questions that stretch your thinking and lead to surprising new insights about the assumptions that drive your behavior. For instance, did you know that your ability to fully partner with others is often blocked not by their resistance, but by your own hidden beliefs? Before you can cultivate truly effective partnerships, there is some essential groundwork you must do on your own. This guide will show you how to move from low collaboration to high collaboration. Of course, the other part of the equation is understanding others. In this book you'll learn about the unconscious attitudes that govern the ways white men do – and don't – participate in diversity efforts. You'll even discover why it's difficult for white women and people of color to see what white men really know about diversity. (Hint: white men are people, too.) Consider this guide required reading for all white women and people of color who want to work more effectively with white men and others.

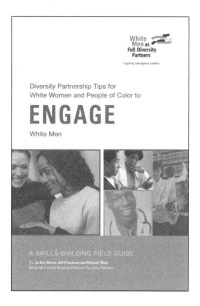

$15.95 ISBN 0-9754192-2-6

order books at www.wmfdp.com

AUTHOR BIOGRAPHIES

MICHAEL WELP, PH.D. is a founding partner of White Men as Full Diversity Partners®. Known for his authentic, trust-building style, Michael works to develop leadership in everyone. Michael has facilitated interracial teambuilding for South African corporations, and has authored a dissertation and book chapter about white men and diversity. An adjunct faculty at the Capella University, he is the recipient of the Minnesota Organization Development Practitioner of the Year Award and is a professional member of NTL Institute for Applied Behavioral Science. Michael also founded EqualVoice, an organization development consulting firm known for building collaborative work cultures and for its transformative approaches to conflict. *He lives in Sandpoint, Idaho and can be reached at 208.263.6775 or welp@wmfdp.com.*

JO ANN MORRIS is a founding partner of White Men as Full Diversity Partners®. She is an executive coach and organization change consultant. Her practice is noted for its Integral Coaching methods for executives and Diversity In-depth Coaching.

Jo Ann was an Information Technology and Programming Manager for 15 years prior to WMFDP. Jo Ann's most challenging technology position was with Fidelity Mutual funds. She was their software programming manager.

She has been a guest lecturer at the Lyndon Baines Johnson Public Executive Institute at the University of Texas at Austin and at the Brandeis University Women in Management Program. She has designed and facilitated diversity initiatives with clients ranging from The Greater Greensboro North Carolina Chamber of Commerce, Exxon Chemicals and Lucent Technologies to the General Services Administration and American Express. *She lives in Connecticut and can be reached at 202.352.4776 or morris@wmfdp.com.*

BILL PROUDMAN is a founding partner of White Men as Full Diversity Partners®, a consulting firm that develops courageous leaders who build effective partnerships between white men, white women, and men and women of color in organizations. He pioneered white-male-only learning labs in the mid-90s after noticing that white male leaders repeatedly disengaged from diversity efforts, almost always looking to white women, and men and women of color, to lead and educate. This provocative work became the seed for his involvement in the creation of WMFDP.

Bill remains an avid diversity learner and an impassioned believer that everyone has a role to play to create just and equitable communities and organizations. He has 25 years experience as a process facilitator and consultant working on the human side of organizational change and transformation. Bill has been an ongoing consultant to the American Leadership Forum having designed and conducted numerous residential leadership development programs since the early 90s. *Bill splits time between homes in Portland, Oregon and the southern Cascades of Washington State. He can be reached at 503-281-5585 or proudman@wmfdp.com.*

ABOUT WMFDP

White Men as Full Diversity Partners® is a culture-change consulting firm. We offer coaching, curriculum design, learning lab intensives and system-wide change opportunities to inspire organizational leadership to make commitments, and to operate with courage when addressing issues related to inclusion and diversity. The leading edge of diversity work involves white men, white women and people of color, partnering with each other to move white men from the sidelines of diversity efforts – to being fully in the midst of these efforts at all levels of the organization. In the end we do three things: build skills, transform mindsets, and create powerful partnerships within the organizations we serve. Visit our website for more about WMFDP.

www.wmfdp.com